Kelly Doudna

Published by SandCastle™, an imprint of ABDO Publishing Company, PO Box 398166, Minneapolis, MN 55439.

Printed in the United States of America, North Mankato, Minnesota.
012001
012014

Cover and interior photo credits: Comstock, Digital Stock, Eyewire, PhotoDisc
Library of Congress Cataloging-in-Publication Data

Doudna, Kelly, 1963-
    Qq / Kelly Doudna.
      p. cm. -- (The alphabet)
    ISBN 1-57765-437-4 (hardcover)
    ISBN 1-59197-017-2 (paperback)
    1. Readers (Primary) [1. Alphabet] I. Title.

   PE1119 .D686 2000
   428.1--dc21

                             00-056899

The SandCastle concept, content, and reading method have been reviewed and approved by a national advisory board including literacy specialists, librarians, elementary school teachers, early childhood education professionals, and parents.

Let Us Know

After reading the book, SandCastle would like you to tell us your stories about reading. What is your favorite page? Was there something hard that you needed help with? Share the ups and downs of learning to read. We want to hear from you! To get posted on the ABDO Publishing Company Web site, send us email at:

sandcastle@abdopublishing.com

About SandCastle™

A professional team of educators, reading specialists, and content developers created the SandCastle™ series to support young readers as they develop reading skills and strategies and increase their general knowledge. The SandCastle™ series has four levels that correspond to early literacy development in young children. The levels are provided to help teachers and parents select the appropriate books for young readers.

Emerging Readers
(no flags)

Beginning Readers
(1 flag)

Transitional Readers
(2 flags)

Fluent Readers
(3 flags)

These levels are meant only as a guide. All levels are subject to change.

To see a complete list of SandCastle™ books and other nonfiction titles from ABDO Publishing Company, visit **www.abdopubublishing.com** or contact us at:

PO Box 398166, Minneapolis, MN 55439

We have fun
playing croquet.

Quinn has a bouquet.

We squint in the
sun.

Quincy sits in squishy mud.

Quico sits quietly.

Quang sits quietly
with Mom.

Queta squirts water all over.

Quentin drinks freshly squeezed juice.

What is Quenna
dressed as?

(queen)

Words I Can Read

Nouns

A noun is a person, place, or thing

bouquet (boh-KAY) p. 7
croquet (kroh-KAY) p. 5
fun (FUHN) p. 5
juice (JOOSS) p. 19
mud (MUHD) p. 11
queen (KWEEN) p. 21
sun (SUHN) p. 9
water (WAW-tur) p. 17

Proper Nouns

A proper noun is the name
of a person, place, or thing

Mom (MOM) p. 15
Quang (KWONG) p. 15
Quenna (KWEN-uh) p. 21
Quentin (KWENT-uhn) p. 19

22

Queta (KAY-tuh) p. 17
Quico (KEE-koh) p. 13
Quincy (KWIN-see) p. 11
Quinn (KWIN) p. 7

Verbs

A verb is an action or being word

dressed (DREST) p. 21
drinks (DRINGK) p. 19
has (HAZ) p. 7
have (HAV) p. 5
is (IZ) p. 21
playing (PLAY-ing) p. 5
sits (SITSS) pp. 11, 13, 15
squint (SKWINT) p. 9
squirts (SKWURT) p. 17

More **Qq** Words

quarter

quilt

square

squirrel

24